GASTON'S
La Jolla

GASTON'S
La Jolla
BY GASTON LOKVIG
Published by CAROL MENDEL

Dedication

*To Jytte Rostrup, my friend--who shares
my love of La Jolla, and has always been so
supportive of my art.*

*To Carol Mendel, my publisher--for her
patience, support, and inspiration.
Without her, this book would not exist.*

*And to Jytte and Tor Lokvig, my daughter
and son--for all the encouragement
they have given me through the years.*

Published by
Carol Mendel
P. O. Box 6022
San Diego, CA 92106

Printed in the
United States of America

ISBN 0-935179-05-4 cloth
ISBN 0-935179-10-0 paper

GASTON--1963

Table of Contents

Introduction

My family and I came to the United States from Denmark in 1959. Although we loved Denmark, my daughter spent a year as an exchange student in the United States, and when she returned she convinced us to move there.

We decided that as long as we were going to emigrate, we would pick a place with better weather. We sailed from Copenhagen to New York, where we bought a car and headed west.

Before long, we arrived in San Diego, and shortly after that I discovered La Jolla. I fell in love.

How can you help falling in love with such a beautiful place as La Jolla?

Soon, I was both living and working there. I had a graphic art studio on Pearl Street, and lived in a little red-brick house on Draper Avenue.

I bought a bicycle, and every morning about 7 a.m. year-round, I'd ride down to La Jolla Cove for a swim.

What a wonderful way to start a day!

Around 1961 I started making pen-and-ink sketches, and I liked it so much I almost forgot about my photography hobby.

Since I lived in La Jolla, and loved it, naturally most of my sketches were of the "village".

Sometimes I look at one of my early illustrations and am sad that what I sketched is no longer there.

On the other hand, there are times when I look at a new building and discover that it excites me so much that I can hardly wait to draw it! La Jolla keeps growing--at times a little too much--but I have tried to keep up with it. One can spend a lifetime just sketching in La Jolla and never finish.

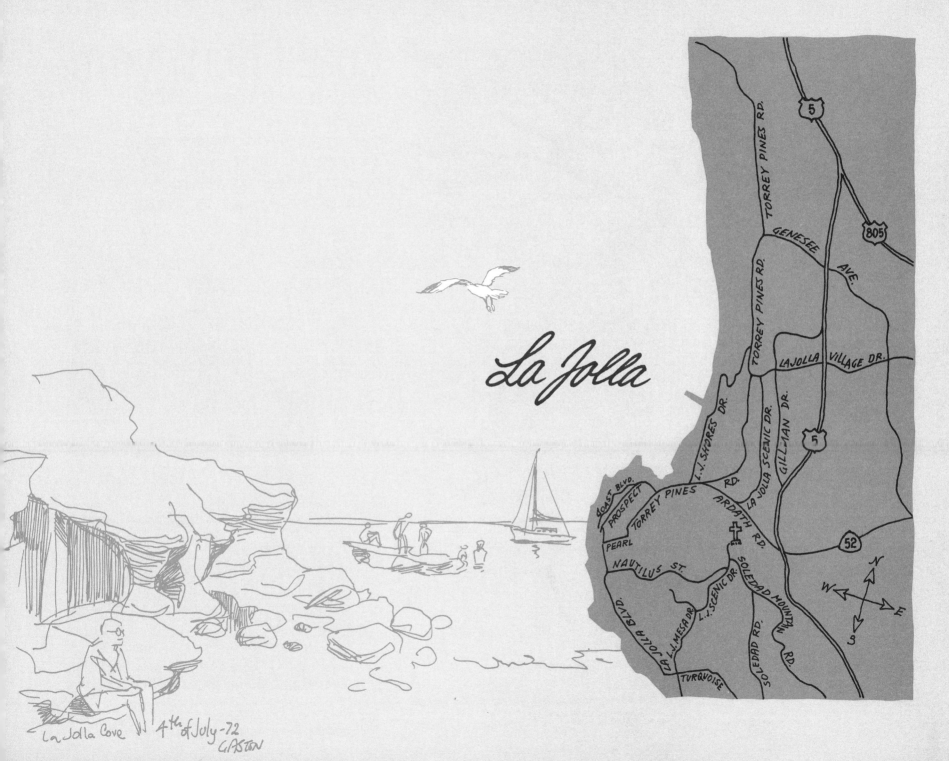

La Jolla

COAST BLVD.
PROSPECT
PEARL
TORREY PINES
NAUTILUS ST.
LA JOLLA BLVD.
TURQUOISE
L.J. MESA DR.
L.J. SCENIC DR.
SOLEDAD RD.
SOLEDAD MOUNTAIN RD.
ARDATH RD.
LA JOLLA SCENIC DR.
L.J. SHORES DR.
RD.
GILLMAN DR.
TORREY PINES RD.
TORREY PINES RD.
LA JOLLA VILLAGE DR.
GENESEE AVE.
5
805
5
52

N
W
E
S

La Jolla Cove   4th of July -72
GASTON

7

Coast Boulevard

Breathtaking views of the Pacific Ocean---pelicans flying overhead---snorkelers and swimmers in La Jolla Cove. Feel the spray as the surf rolls in and breaks against the shore.

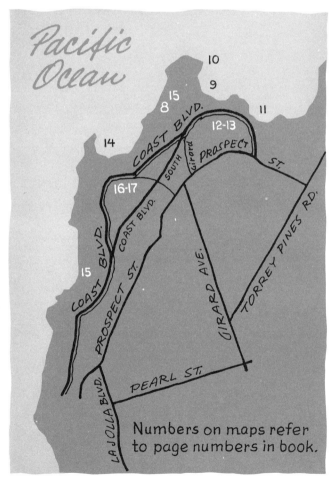

Pacific Ocean

Numbers on maps refer to page numbers in book.

This Monterey cypress tree in Ellen Browning Scripps Park speaks its own language about time, wind and survival.

8

This is one of my first drawings of La Jolla, made during the years when I lived in La Jolla and swam in the Cove daily.

NO FLOATS OR SPEARS IN COVE

GASTON— 1969

La Jolla Cove

Alligator Head was once a
La Jolla landmark. It doesn't
look like this anymore,
because the arch collapsed
during a 1977 storm.

GASTON - 1969

La Jolla Cave and Shell Shop

There are many caves along the cliffs here, and you can enter one of them through this shop.

Alligator Head

When I began this drawing, it was low tide. I was sitting on a rock with only my feet in the water.
As I sat there sketching, the water got higher and higher. By the time I finished the drawing I was sitting in water, struggling to keep the waves from splashing onto the drawing.

"The Clam"

Daredevils like to jump off this cliff. It's dangerous and there are signs against it, but they do it anyway.

◄ *Red Rest*
The Red Rest is one of a group of "California bungalows" that were built here in the 1890's.

GASTON-
1986

13

14

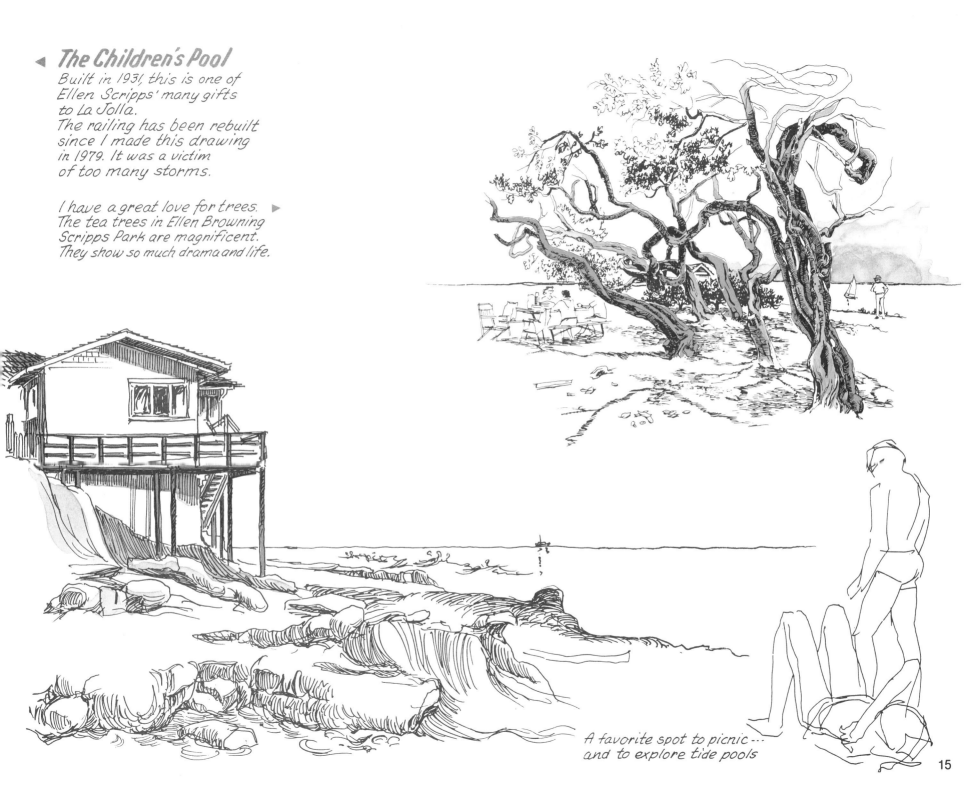

The Children's Pool

Built in 1931, this is one of
Ellen Scripps' many gifts
to La Jolla.
The railing has been rebuilt
since I made this drawing
in 1979. It was a victim
of too many storms.

I have a great love for trees. ▶
The tea trees in Ellen Browning
Scripps Park are magnificent.
They show so much drama and life.

A favorite spot to picnic...
and to explore tide pools

15

Casa de Mañana

The Casa de Mañana, built in
the early 1920's, was a prominent
La Jolla hotel for 30 years.
Now it is a retirement home.
The sketch at left is from
the back, so you see the side
of the buildings and also a little
of the water.

The larger drawing shows the
superb view of the Pacific Ocean.
I sketched here 5 or 6 times
before I found the best positions
for my drawings.

GASTON—
May 1978

GASTON-
-86

17

A canopy invites you into one of
Prospect Street's many restaurants.

GASTON—

Prospect Street

Restaurants··· art galleries···
boutiques. Everywhere you
look there are people walking
around enjoying themselves.

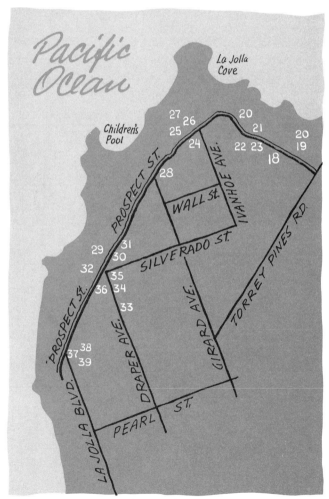

Coast Walk

I like this shopping center very much. There used to be small cottages here, which eventually became shops. They were torn down in 1976 to build Coast Walk, which maintains the flavor of the original cottages.

Hunan Garden RESTAURANT

Coast Walk

UNDERGROUND PARKING BELOW

GASTON-
1984.

19

GASTON

I love stuffed animals!

A nice combination of columns, lamps, and palm tree. I had to shorten the palm tree to fit it into this drawing.

Green Dragon Colony ▶

These buildings started out as cottages at the turn of the century. In the late 1940's they were converted and expanded to the complex you see today. Unfortunately, the giant eucalyptus tree is now gone.

LA JOLLA ZOO
Stuffed Toys

International Shops

Prospect Street is always changing. I made the drawing at left just a week before the old facade was torn down. The new look is shown above. The drawing to the right shows the back of the courtyard inside. It's my favorite spot here, and hasn't changed much.

dos pescados
hand wrought jewelry

The Silver Box

La Jolla Sandwich

GASTON-

A street scene along Prospect ▶
in front of La Valencia Hotel.
This area along Prospect Street
is always busy.

◀ Such a charming round roof!
I always think of this as The
Turntable, from the many years
it was a record store. That's La
Valencia Hotel in the background.

Ivanhoe   Prospect

25

◄ La Valencia Hotel

This prestigious hotel was
built in the late 1920's.
Its pink stucco walls and red
tile roof make it a La Jolla landmark.

A handsome bronze sculpture ►
by Francisco Zuniga keeps watch
over the hotel's outdoor restaurant.

GASTON 1979

The old and the new

To the left is an example of the new and exciting architecture along *Prospect*. It is bursting with fun and imagination. On the right is one of La Jolla's early wood cottages, built in 1905.

I love them both.

I often do rough sketches like this before making a final drawing.

Saint James-By-The-Sea ▶

This church is made up of so many interesting buildings!
It was a pleasure to draw it.

◀ This fountain is in the front of Saint James-By-The-Sea. I never knew how beautiful it was until I sat down to sketch it.

CHAPEL

GASTON-70

31

GASTON - 1969

◄ *La Jolla Museum of Contemporary Art*

*The pattern here is circles and straight lines---
straight lines in the columns, circles in the concrete
on the sidewalks. The sunshine through the trees
adds to the overall pleasing effect.*

The Bed and Breakfast Inn at La Jolla

*This home was designed by Irving Gill, an architect
well known in Southern California for his simplified
California mission style. Built in 1913, the home has
recently been converted to a bed-and-breakfast house.*

▼

GASTON-
NOV. 1985.

La Jolla Woman's Club

In the drawing on the left, the tree seems to protect the building.

The drawing on the right shows the main entrance, on Silverado. The building was designed by Irving Gill and built in 1913.

GASTON-
Oct. 1979.

WOMAN'S CLUB

715

GASTON-

La Jolla Recreation Center

This building was also
designed by Irving Gill.
There is a charming fountain
and sculpture in the foreground.

GASTON-
Oct. 1979.

The Bishop's School

The Bishop's School is
a private school for grades
7-12. It recently celebrated
its 75th anniversary.

YIELD

◄ A quick sketch, in the courtyard facing the dining area

The Bishop's School
◄ A view of the chapel from the courtyard

The main entrance ►

39

Girard Avenue

Big stores, little stores, old buildings, new buildings, buildings under construction---Girard is the main commercial street of La Jolla and contains a variety of all there is in La Jolla.

GASTON-

Entrance to Seville condominiums.

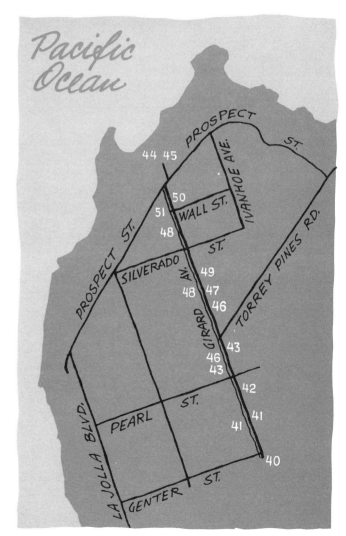

La Jolla Elementary School
The beautiful trees add shade and life to the plain facade of the school.

Professional Building ▶
Spanish-style architecture is popular in La Jolla. I find this example particularly appealing.

La Jolla Elementary School

GASTON
oct. 1983

41

The Hairstylists

girard TRAVEL

PANNIKIN COFFEE TEA SPICE

Pannikin

A popular place to meet your friends. The strong coffee here reminds me of the coffee that's served in Europe.

GASTON-1983

42

Harry's COFFEE shop

QUALITY CLEANERS

7547

MAR. 86

GASTON-

SAFEWAY
PARKING ▶

RIGHT
TURN
ONLY

Quality
CLEANERS

BO-DANICA IMPORTS

phones

*Familiar sights
along Girard*

View from Girard and Prospect

44

This drawing started out as a sketch of the delightful buildings on the left. I later decided to turn the drawing into a panorama.

GASTON-
1981

GASTON-
Aug 1981

▲

I drew this little flower shop, "bloomers," when it was on Ivanhoe Ave. Now it's on Girard beside Saks Fifth Avenue.

◄ *The Stuards building has been torn down since this was drawn.*

Mary, Star of the Sea ►

I like this Spanish-style church--- the building shapes, the chapel, the mosaic, the bell, everything.

GASTON-

47

Girard Avenue ▶

This drawing wasn't planned.
I was waiting for someone
and decided to do a street scene
while I waited.

◀ **Warwick's**

These shoppers are looking into
the window of La Jolla's oldest
business, founded in 1902.

Cove Theatre

The Cove Theater is an important
part of La Jolla. The arch at the
entrance is quite distinctive.
▼

San Dieg

Adelaide's

La Jolla Public Library

We're looking down Wall Street.
The Spanish-style building on
the corner is the public library.

STOP
AHEAD

WALL ST
GIRARD AVE

50

Arcade Building

My thanks to architect Herbert Palmer for designing this charming little building. We're looking across Girard Avenue, down Wall Street.

OPEN

John's Waffle Shop

WALL & GIRARD AVE

GASTON—

51

La Jolla Light

Corner of Wall St. and Ivanhoe

GASTON

The Village

You can easily walk everywhere, and always find delightful surprises. I hope La Jolla maintains its "village" atmosphere.

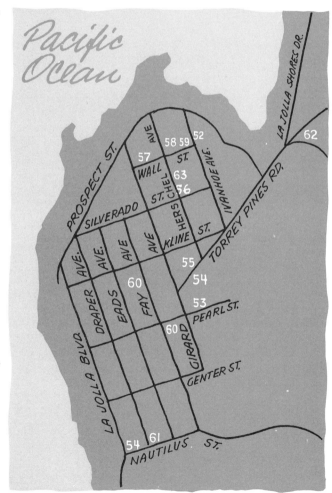

Pearl Street

For many years I had my art studio in the building at the left edge of this drawing, at the corner of Pearl and Girard.

The building in the foreground is a professional building.

GASTON

A secluded entrance framed
by giant bird-of-paradise plants.

◀ Such beautiful landscaping!
I love the pretty fountain and pool.

I like all the wood in this ▶
shopping center at the corner of
Herschel Ave. and Torrey Pines Road.

54

The Bottle Shop

Wine Bar

GASTON-

The picket fence looks so good against the bricks.

Athenaeum

The Athenaeum is a private music and arts library on Wall St. On the left side of the drawing is the La Jolla branch of the public library.

GASTON–

La Jolla Post Office

The Spanish-style building is nicely shaded by trees.
It took me a long time to make the drawing on the left,
because I was standing in the street and had to move
every time a car wanted to drive up to the mailbox.

Village Galleria

I sketched this while the building
was under construction.
I think it will be charming and
playful when it's finished.
I look forward to walking around in it.

◄ Sycamore Court

Surrounded by trees and flowers,
Sycamore Court is as romantic as
the Village Galleria is playful.

La Jolla High School ►

My favorite view of the school
is from Draper Avenue,
because of the combination
of steps, trees, and plants.

◄ New Fire Station

The building looks so non-commercial---
almost like a home!
The day I drew it, there wasn't
a fire truck in the driveway.
I came back a different day to get it.

Old Fire Station

This is at the corner of Herschel and Wall.
The Spanish-style building in the center
used to be the La Jolla Fire Station.
▼

Residential Areas

What a variety of homes you find in La Jolla! --- from Tudor to Spanish; from bungalows to modern. I love to explore the area.

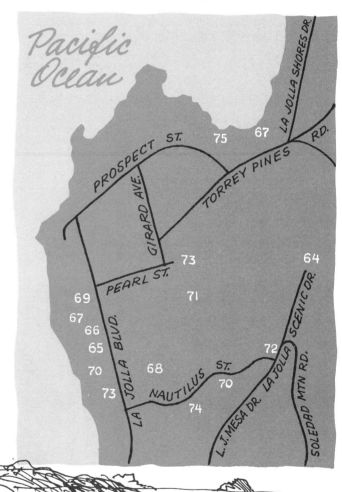

A rough sketch of the cross at the top of Mount Soledad. I made a more "finished" sketch too, but I liked the rough sketch better. It gives more of the impression of the place.

La Jolla has many homes that were designed by architects as their own homes. This home, built in the 1920's, is a beautiful example. The architect was Edgar Ullrich, who also designed Casa de Mañana.

GASTON

Architect Herbert Palmer designed
this as his home. Its resemblance to
India's Taj Mahal earned it the nickname "Taj."

A charming Tudor-style home
nestles behind the trees.

Monterey cypress trees add drama
to this gracious Spanish-style home. ▶

GASTON - 1981

I lived near this home for many years and have always liked it.

DRAPER AVE.
←7100

GASTON- '86

League House

This apartment house is run by the Social Service League of La Jolla.

Darlington House ▶

The Darlington House also belongs to the Social Service League. It is a popular site for weddings and parties. Proceeds benefit the League House.

1451

Hillside homes along Nautilus Street.

I just liked the Chimney and antenna on this little house.

A lovely half-timbered home.

There is no lack of fantasies when it comes to mailboxes on Nautilus Street.

La Jolla Country Club

A lovely location for a country club.
The view of La Jolla from here is marvelous.

PARKING
PRO SHOP
LOCKER ROOMS
→

GASTON
-86

71

When I'm on my way
to Mount Soledad,
I know I'm going the
right way
when I pass this church.

All Hallows Catholic Church

GASTON-1986

A cozy home
tucked away
on a side street

Homes perched
on the steep hillside
at the base
of Mount Soledad

I can keep on
sketching half-timbered
houses all over La Jolla
and never get tired of it.

GASTON '74

GASTON - 1980

"The Silver Ship"

If this reminds you,
     as it did me,
of a combination of a ship
and something from outer space,
you're on the right track.
Architect Eugene Ray had
these ideas in mind when
he designed this as his home
and studio.

     On a practical level, he
was also thinking about
economical ways to build
a home with large, open
interior spaces on a lot
with a 23% slope.

Many La Jolla homes ▶
sit on cliffs overlooking
the Pacific Ocean.
     You can take a spectacular
walk along "Coast Walk,"
a path in front of these homes.

La Jolla Shores

I love the beach at La Jolla Shores. When I'm finished playing in the ocean with my boogie board, I take a stroll along Avenida de la Playa.

AQUARIUM

Scripps Aquarium

A tide pool exhibit complete with tides and waves welcomes visitors to Scripps Aquarium.

Scripps Institution of Oceanography ▶

Scripps Institution
of Oceanography
is one of the world's
foremost centers
for marine research.
It is part of the
University of
California.
Here you see the Marine
Biology Building.

◀ Scripps Pier

Scripps research vessels
dock at the end of this pier.
Under the pier
is a popular beach.

SAN DIEGO MARINE LIFE
UNLAWFUL TO TAKE

GASTON
-86.

79

La Jollans just love to build houses on the edges of cliffs and hillsides!

GASTON-
1984

Marine Room
This popular restaurant
is at the water's edge.
It is adjacent to the
La Jolla Beach and Tennis Club.

GASTON-
Feb. '85

The Enchanted Cottage

Gift Shop

SEIKO Boutique

SEIKO Bell JAPANESE GIFTS

SEIKO Originals

DRESSMAKING ALTERATIONS

LAW OFFICES

GASTON-'83

The Rheinlander Restaurant

For many, many years The Rheinlander was a landmark
on Avenida de la Playa. Fortunately, I made a drawing
of it in 1983. Since then it has been replaced by another
fine restaurant, Gustaf Anders, and looks entirely different.

◄ Avenida de la Playa is lined with small shops.
This building is my favorite.
Architecturally there is so much going on.

Dec. 1983
GASTON—

Avenida de la Playa

I started out planning to draw only the part on the right---
the tree and the cars. I kept adding to it---
and soon I had the whole street.

I like to eat at small deli's,
like the one here on Avenida
de la Playa.

Torrey Pines Mesa

This area is developing rapidly. Set aside from all the bustle are the beautiful Torrey pine trees for which the area is named.

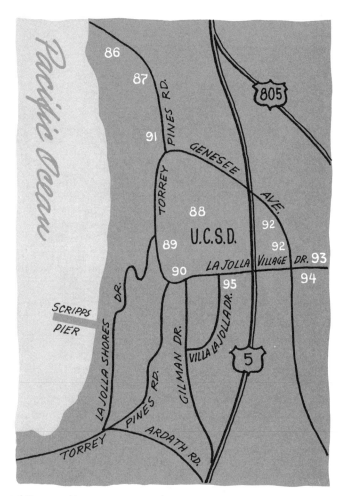

Pacific Ocean

86
87
91
805
GENESEE AVE.
TORREY PINES RD.
88
U.C.S.D.
92
89
92
LA JOLLA VILLAGE DR. 93
90
94
95
SCRIPPS PIER
LA JOLLA SHORES DR.
VILLA LA JOLLA DR.
GILMAN DR.
5
TORREY PINES RD.
ARDATH RD.
TORREY

◄ Nice paths invite you to walk around and enjoy the trees at Torrey Pines State Reserve.

Torrey Pines Golf Course

The Andy Williams golf tournament is held here every February.
I love the handsome Torrey pine that stands beside the pro shop.

GASTON-
86

GASTON-
198

University of California at San Diego

U.C.S.D. is one of nine campuses of the University of California, and is made up of several colleges.

◄ Central University Library serves all the colleges. It is surrounded by eucalyptus trees, and the lines of the building blend well with the lines of the trees.

The architectural style of each ► campus is different. I especially like the buildings on the campus of Revelle College. This began as a rough sketch, but then turned into the final drawing.

GASTON

◀ Mandell Weiss Center for the Performing Arts

You can go around this theater at U.C.S.D. and see new lines all the time. This position shows the most lines of the architecture.

Scripps Clinic and Research Foundation

This famous medical center began with a gift from Ellen Scripps in 1924.

▼

GREEN
HOSPITAL

Scripp's Clinic

Marriott

4320

GIRARD Savings Ba

Computerland

Golden Triangle

The "Golden Triangle" is the area bounded by I-5, I-805, and Route 52.
This is a quick sketch showing a few of the many new buildings that are going up in this area.

La Jolla Plaza, seen from the northwest corner of University Towne Centre.

La Jolla Country Day School

This fountain of a water mill reminds me of the many water mills I have seen in my native Denmark.

Outpost   Levi's

The
CHILDREN'S
MUSEUM

◄ *University Towne Centre*

*The architecture at U.T.C.
is enormously appealing
to me. I always feel good
when I am there. Drawing
this was pure pleasure.*

La Jolla Village Square ▶

*The Children's Museum
of San Diego is on the
ground floor of this
shopping center.
I had fun framing it
with the pushcart and
plants that sit nearby.*

95

Index

About the Artist

Gaston Lokvig, a native of Denmark, started his graphic arts career in Copenhagen. For many years he worked in lithography and rotogravure for some of the largest printing companies in Copenhagen.

His technical experience, combined with his exceptional artistic talent, won him the position of art director for one of Denmark's leading magazines. Soon he was also illustrating children's books and drawing film posters for such major studios as M.G.M., Walt Disney, and Warner Brothers.

In 1959 he came to California, discovered San Diego, and stayed here to work as a free-lance graphic artist. Soon he was living in La Jolla, and using his spare time to create pen-and-ink illustrations.

Gaston's work is featured on note cards, maps, and books about the San Diego area. This book contains illustrations of La Jolla drawn over the last twenty years.